'I am glad I am American.

I am glad I am free.

But, I wish I was a dog, and Bill Clinton was a tree.'

Also by Iain Dale and published by Robson Books

As I Said to Denis: The Margaret Thatcher Book of Quotations
The Blair Necessities: The Tony Blair Book of Quotations
The Unofficial Book of Political Lists

The Bill Clinton Joke Book – *Uncensored*

Iain Dale
and
John Simmons

For Daniel Forrester
and Tracey and Martyn Meek

First published in Great Britain in 1998 by Robson Books Ltd, Bolsover House, 5-6 Clipstone Street, London W1P 8LE

British Library Cataloguing in Publication Data
A catalogue record for this title is available from the British Library

ISBN 1 86105 194 8

Printed in Great Britain by
St Edmundsbury Press Limited, Bury St Edmunds, Suffolk

Foreword

It's about time Bill Clinton was taken seriously. No, really. He is, after all, leader of the free world. But he is also the subject of scandal, intrigue and gossip like few presidents before him. He cites Kennedy as his hero and he seems to have done a pretty good job in emulating him both in terms of the size of his libido and also as a worse than average president.

It is now a national pastime in the United States to poke (and we use the word advisedly) fun at the President. His alleged sexual antics have distracted him and his administration from their task of governing and have led to him becoming a joke to most of the world. Yet unlike most politicians he gets away with it. Despite being among the most puritanical of peoples, the American people appear to have forgiven Bill Clinton for his misdemeanours and regard him as nothing worse than a bit of a rogue. Despite the nightly attacks from Messers Leno, Letterman and O'Brien (to whom our thanks go also) the mud just doesn't stick.

We have tried to make this book accessible to all, including those who haven't followed every minute of Clinton's life, particularly in Britain. Given our subject, there are bound to be a few jokes where the reader raises a quizzical eyebrow; so to those who haven't remembered Clinton's admission of drug taking – 'But I didn't inhale', or heart- (or is it gut) rendering – 'I feel your pain' quote, just remember that most of the jokes in this book can either be traced back to inhaling, feeling pain or sexual antics of one kind or another (including the reputation of Clinton's home state Arkansas for being a place where the family trees don't fork too often!). All in the best *possible* taste, of course!

We would like to thank all those whose material has contributed to this book. In particular, our thanks go to Jeremy Robson and his colleagues at Robson Books, to Celena Carden for her inspiration and to Bill and Hillary for giving us all so much to make fun of.

We soon hope to publish a new collection of jokes about all aspects of political life. If you have any political jokes you think we should include, please write to us at Robson Books, Bolsover House, 5-6 Clipstone Street, London, W1, England.

No doubt there will be those who have a collective sense of humour by-pass when they read parts of this book. Shame.

Iain Dale
John Simmons
March 1998

Who's Who
&
What's What
in Bill's Life

Arkansas
One of the poorest and smallest states in the USA, which Bill is proud to call home. He loves to wax lyrical about his hard upbringing in a small town called Hope. He served two terms as Governor of Arkansas before embarking on his Presidential campaign.

George Bush
Bill Clinton beat Bush to become President. Bush was famous for saying 'Read my lips – no new taxes'. Two years later he raised taxes and probably lost the election to Clinton because of it.

Bill Clinton
All-powerful President of the United States and former Governor of America's 'hickest' state, Arkansas. Known for his alleged drug use while at university in England (although he maintains he didn't 'inhale') and for his serial philandering.

Hillary Rodham Clinton
Bill's feisty First Lady who insists on using her maiden name 'Rodham'. A lawyer by training, Bill no doubt uses her for some useful free advice. Hillary was a staffer at the Nixon Watergate hearings in 1973. She is said to have amassed a fortune through fortunate share dealings. Wrote a book called *It Takes a Village*.

Chelsea Clinton
Teenage First Daughter recently shipped off to Seattle to go to university. Renowned for being 'stir -fried in the ugly wok', Chelsea's looks can only improve with age.

Bob Dole
Respected Second World War veteran, former Republican Senate Majority Leader and presidential candidate who stood against a draft-dodging, serial philanderering former Governor from a small state and lost...Life just ain't fair sometimes!

Gennifer Flowers
First of Bill's 'Bimbo Eruptions'. Her revelations of an affair in 1992 threatened to scupper Clinton's presidential campaign but he survived – just. Flowers has since been a thorn in the Clinton's side and has even appeared in *Playboy*.

Vince Foster
Friend of the Clintons who became Chief Counsel to the President. His apparent suicide in the White House led to all sorts of rumours about his relationship with the First Lady and various conspiracy theories.

Al Gore
Bill's Vice President with a wife called Tipper. Gore was a senator from Tennessee and is renowned for his woodenness. Considers himself an environmental expert. Aims to succeed Bill as President in the year 2000.

Paula Jones
Arkansas woman who alleges Bill Clinton exposed himself to her and asked her for oral sex. Currently

involved in a lawsuit against the President, who denies everything.

Monica Lewinsky
As a 19 year old intern at the White House, Monica appears to have had more access to the President than she could ever have dreamed. She told a friend, Linda Tripp, about her sexual liaisons with the President. Coincidentally Tripp recorded the whole conversation on tape and presented the evidence to Kenneth Starr, the Special Prosecutor into the Clinton's Whitewater dealings. Nice to have friends...

Socks & Buddy
The White House cat and dog.

Whitewater
Piece of real estate in Arkansas which Hillary and Bill invested in, and made a killing. So much of a killing that the Senate has convened hearings which could lead to the Clintons being indicted.

Kenneth Starr
Supposed Independent Special Prosecutor who is the bain of the Clintons. Led the Whitewater investigations and now seems to have set himself up as chief investigator into Clinton's sex life too.

The Long & the Short of It

President Clinton brought his new dog into the West Wing. It was a disaster. He ate everything in sight, sniffed the crotches of all the secretaries and humped the legs of all the interns. And Buddy didn't behave too well either.

President Clinton and the Pope died on the same day, and due to an administrative mix up, Clinton was sent to heaven and the Pope went to hell.

The Pope explained the situation to the devil, he checked out all of the paperwork, and the error was acknowledged. The Pope was told, however, that it would take about 24 hours to fix the problem and correct the error.

The next day, the Pope was called in and the devil said his good-bye as he went off to heaven. On his way up, he met Clinton who was on his way down, and they stopped to chat.

Pope: Sorry about the mix up.
President Clinton: No problem.
Pope: Well, I'm really excited about going to heaven.
President Clinton: Why's that?
Pope: All my life I've wanted to meet the Virgin Mary.
President Clinton: You're a day late.

At a doctors' convention in Switzerland, a conversation was taking place at a local tavern after an enthusiastic mid-day lecture. A Jewish doctor said, 'Medicine in my country is so advanced that we can take a kidney out of one person and put it in another, and have him looking for work in 6 weeks.' A German doctor said, 'That's nothing! In Germany we can take a lung out of one person and put it in another, and have him looking for work in 4 weeks!' A Russian doctor chipped in, 'In my country, medicine is so advanced that we can take half of a heart from one person and put it in another, and have them both looking for work in two weeks!'

The American doctor, not to be outdone, said, 'HAH! We can take an asshole out of Arkansas, put him in the White House, and have half of the country looking for work the next day!'

Bill and Hillary are at a restaurant. The waiter tells them tonight's special is chicken almondine and fresh fish. 'The chicken sounds good; I'll have that,' Hillary says.

The waiter nods. 'And the vegetable?' he asks.

'Oh, he'll have the fish,' Hillary replies.

Bill Clinton returns from a vacation in Arkansas and walks down the steps of Air Force One with two pigs under his arms. At the bottom of the steps, the honor guardsman steps forward and remarks, 'Nice pigs, Mr President.'

Clinton replies, 'I'll have you know that these are genuine Arkansas Razor Back Hogs. I got this one for Chelsea and this one for Hillary. So, now what do you think?'

The honor guardsman answers: 'Nice trade, Sir.'

Senator Bob Kerrey, when asked about Bill Clinton evading the draft:

'Do I care if he evaded the draft? Well, a part of me does.'

[*Bob Kerrey lost an arm in Vietnam.*]

The new definition of silence: Quayle and Clinton telling their Vietnam War stories to each other.

A man was walking along the street when he spotted a small boy busily constructing something. He approached the boy and was shocked to see him playing with cow manure! For lack of anything better to say, he asked, 'Little boy, what ARE you doing?'

The boy replied, 'I am making George Bush, mister.'

Now, thoroughly taken aback, the man asked, 'Why are you making George Bush? Why not make, er, Bill Clinton?'

The boy answered, 'Oh no mister, I can't make Bill Clinton.'

'But why not?' asked the man.

The boy replied 'Well, mister, there isn't enough bullshit here to make Bill Clinton.'

One day Bill Clinton was out jogging. Suddenly he tripped over a rock and fell from a bridge into a very cold river.

Three boys, playing along the riverbank, saw the accident and without a thought, jumped in the water and dragged the wet President out.

After cleaning himself up he said: 'Boys, you saved the President of the United States. You deserve a reward. You name it, I'll give it to you.'

The first boy said: 'Please, I'd like a ticket to Disneyland!'

'I'll personally hand it to you,' said Mr Clinton.

'I'd like a pair of Nike Air Turbos,' the second boy said.

'I'll buy them myself and give them to you,' said the grateful defender of the Western Hemisphere.

'And I'd like a wheelchair with a stereo in it,' said the third boy.

'I'll personally ... wait a second ... you're not even handicapped!'

'No, but I will be when my father finds out who I saved from drowning.'

While Bill, Hillary and Chelsea were vacationing in Wyoming, the housekeeper was tasked with looking after their pet parrot. They hadn't been gone for more than a couple of days when the parrot was found dead in the bottom of its cage.

The housekeeper set out to find a replacement bird and visited nearly every pet store in Washington. After several hours of looking, she came across an exact duplicate of the bird. As she purchased the parrot, the shop owner cautioned her that the bird had previously been owned by a Madam and had lived for several years in a house of ill-repute. The housekeeper said that no one would ever know and took the bird back to the White House.

The morning after the Clintons returned to the White House, Chelsea walked through the room and the bird said, 'Too young.'

A little later Hillary came into the room and the bird responded with, 'Too old.'

That afternoon the President entered the room and the bird said, 'HI BILL!'

The Clinton campaign slogan 'It's the Economy, Stupid!' has been replaced by a new sign hanging behind the desk in the Oval Office. It reads: 'I Never Said That.'

Bill and Hillary are at the first baseball game of the season. The umpire walks up to the VIP section and yells something. Suddenly Clinton grabs Hillary by the collar and throws her over the side and onto the field.

The stunned umpired shouts, 'No, Mr President! I said, "Throw the first PITCH!" '

President Clinton looks up from his desk in the Oval Office to see one of his aides nervously approach him.

'What is it?' exclaims the President.

'It's this Abortion Bill Mr President, what do you want to do about it?' the aide replies.

'Just go ahead and pay it,' responds the President.

Clinton is looking out of the window and he notices that someone has urinated the message, 'BILL SUCKS!' on the White House lawn. Furious, he orders the FBI to take urine and handwriting samples from every one of the White House staff and find the culprit immediately.

A week later, the FBI director calls: 'Mr President, I have good news and bad news,' he says. 'The good news is that the urine belongs to Al Gore.'

'And the bad news?' Clinton demands nervously.

After a slight pause, the director replies, 'Sir, er, the handwriting belongs to your wife!'

It's 2:00 am, and Mr Clinton arrives home late.

Hillary: Damn it, Bill, where have you been?!

Bill: Out in the White House garden fertilizing my Flowers.

One day, while being driven around the capitol, Hillary notices a young girl with a wagon full of kittens. On the lookout for a PR event, she stops to talk to the girl. As Hillary admires the kittens, the girl proudly boasts, 'All my kittens are Democrats!'

Hillary thinks this is just the thing to show those nasty Republicans that even little children know the best Party. She makes plans with the little girl to meet

in a couple days with Bill and the press corps. When they meet, Bill kneels down in front of the girl and picks up a kitten. 'Hillary says you have something special to tell me about your kittens,' he says.

'Yes, sir. All my kittens are Republicans!'

Hillary splutters 'You told me they were all Democrats!'

The girl responds, 'Yes ma'am, but that was before they opened their eyes.'

Dan Quayle, Bob Dole, and Bill Clinton are travelling in a car together in the midwest. A tornado comes along and whirls them up into the air and tosses them thousands of yards away. When they come to and extract themselves from the vehicle, they realize they're in the Land of Oz. They decide to go see the Wizard of Oz. Quayle says, 'I'm going to ask the Wizard for a brain.' Dole says, 'I'm going to ask the Wizard for a heart.' Clinton says, 'Where's Dorothy??'

A new Gallup poll asked 1,000 women if they would have sex with Clinton. 70 per cent said, 'Never again.'

In light of all the news about Clinton and 'Oralgate,' the Pope has summoned the College of Cardinals to see about adding an eleventh commandment to the list: Thou shalt not show thy rod to thy staff.

Arkansas is very proud of Clinton – all these women coming forward and none of them is his sister!

Bill Clinton, Bob Dole and Ross Perot are on a long flight in Air Force One. Perot pulls out a $100 bill and says 'I'm going to throw this $100 bill out and make someone down below happy.'

Dole, not wanting to be outdone, says, 'If that was my $100 bill, I would split it into two $50 bills and make two people down below happy.'

Of course Clinton doesn't want these two candidates to outdo him, so he chimes in, 'I would instead take 100 $1 bills and throw them out to make 100 people just a little happier.'

At this point the pilot, who has overheard all this bragging and can't stand it anymore, comes out and says, 'I think I'll throw all three of you out of this plane and make 250 million people happy.'

Hillary and Bill were on vacation one weekend and decided to go for a drive through the beautiful American countryside. After a while, they needed to stop for gas. They pulled into the tiny gas station, and out walked a man to help them. Hillary looked up and screamed at the top of her lungs, 'Oh my God! Charley? Is that you? I can't believe it!'

She leapt out of the car and gave the man a big hug and proceeded to talk with him for a long time. After they were finished talking, they hugged again and Hillary got back in the car.

As they were driving away, Bill turned to Hillary and asked, 'Honey, who was that?'

'That was Charley, an old boyfriend of mine,' she responded. 'We dated for a long time, and almost got married.'

'Oh,' said Bill. 'Well, I guess you're glad you married me instead.'

'Why do you say that?' asked Hillary.

'Because he's only a gas station attendant, and I'm the President of the United States,' exclaimed Bill.

'I don't see how that has anything to do with anything.' said Hillary. 'If I'd married Charley, HE'D be the President!'

When Bill Clinton and Al Gore were first elected, Gore gave Clinton three envelopes and said, 'When you get in trouble, open the first envelope.' Sure enough, a couple of months in office and along comes the Whitewater scandal.

Clinton opens the first envelope and it reads, 'Appoint an independent consul to bury the problem.'

This works for a few years then the campaign financing scandal breaks. So Clinton opens the second envelope. One word, 'Lie!' A short while later Monica Lewinsky pops up. Clinton in a panic opens the final envelope. 'Introduce President Gore.'

President Clinton met with the Chinese Premier and both sides agreed to a compromise. The Chinese president promised to work on human rights, and Clinton promised he wouldn't send Hillary there anymore.

Bill is out jogging one evening and passes a hooker on a street corner. He stops and asks how much. She says $100. He says all he has is $10 and moves on. Next evening, Bill and Hillary are out walking and pass by the same hooker. She shouts, 'SEE WHAT YOU GET FOR $10!'

One day Bill Clinton and the Pope were having a special meeting. For security reasons, they sat in a rowing boat in the middle of a lake, with secret service agents and fans standing all along the shore. While the Pope and Bill were talking, a gust of wind came along and blew the Pope's little white hat off. 'No problem,' said Bill, 'I'll take care of it.' And with that he climbed out of the boat, walked across the water, retrieved the Pope's hat, and returned it to him! The Pope was most startled by this event, but from the shoreline, a voice piped up: 'See? He can't even SWIM!'

Bill Clinton is a president for our times, a truly composite president. He has the hormones of John F. Kennedy, the scruples of Richard Nixon and the memory of Ronald Reagan.

A guy dies and goes to heaven. It's a slow day for St. Peter, so upon passing the entrance test, St. Peter says, 'I'm not very busy today, why don't you let me show you around.'

The guy thinks this is a great idea and graciously accepts the offer. St. Peter shows him all the sights; the golf course, the reading room and the library, the observation room, the cafeteria and then finally, they

come to a HUGE room full of clocks. The guys asks, 'What's up with those clocks?'

St. Peter explains, 'Everyone on earth has a clock that shows how much time he has left on earth. When a clock runs out of time, the person dies and comes to the Gates to be judged.' The guy thinks this makes sense, but noticing that some of the clocks are going faster than others, he asks, 'Why is that?'

St. Peter explains, 'Every time a living person tells a lie, it speeds up his clock.'

This also makes sense, so the guy takes one last look around the room before leaving and notices one clock in the center of the ceiling. On this clock, both hands are spinning at an unbelievable rate. So he asks, 'What's the story with that clock?'

'Oh, that,' St. Peter replies, 'That's Bill Clinton's clock. We decided to use it as a fan.'

If character is not an issue, why isn't Ted Kennedy President?

Oxymoron of the year: Clinton character assassination.

Air Force One crashes, instantly killing President Clinton, Vice President Gore and their wives. Being the very important people that they are, St. Peter greets them personally at the Pearly Gates and informs them that they have been granted an audience with God. They are lead by St. Peter to a tremendous throne room. The Supreme Being, of course, is seated upon the throne.

'And who might you be?' God asks of the Vice President.

'I am Albert Gore Jr, Vice President of the United States of America.'

'Ah, yes. You have done much for the environment. Love your work. Come sit on my left. And you there, who are you?'

'Your holiness, I am William Jefferson Clinton, President of the United States.'

'Right. You are a brave man who has confronted some difficult issues. Come sit on my right. Now, who might you be?'

'My name is Hillary Rodham Clinton and YOU are sitting in MY seat.'

Bill Clinton's out horse-riding when he hears someone shout, 'Hey, look at the prick on that horse!' When he gets home, he takes a look and realizes he's been riding a mare.

☆

Hillary came into the room with a big smile and a spring in her step. 'My, you're in a good mood,' said Bill. 'Why are you so happy?'

'I just got back from my annual physical exam and the doctor said I had the breasts of a 25 year old woman,' Hillary gushed.

'Did he say anything about your 46 year old ass?' Bill asked.

'No,' said Hillary, 'your name wasn't mentioned once.'

Ballot counting in Arkansas... Among the thousands of Clinton ballots, they see a single Bush ballot. 'Put it aside,' says the chief counter. A few hours later they see another Bush ballot. The chief smiles: 'Just as I thought, the Republican bastard has voted twice! Annul both his votes.'

Bill Clinton, George Bush, and Ronald Reagan are in a boat in the Potomac, when suddenly the boat develops a leak. They have only one life preserver jacket. Bill says: 'Let's do the Democratic thing... Take a vote to see who gets the life preserver.' They each write a name on a piece of paper and stuff it in a coffee can. Bush and Reagan get one vote each; Clinton gets six.

A guy goes into a jewellery store looking to buy a watch. He looks at a watch called the George Bush Watch and asks the sales clerk why there are no hands. The sales clerk says, 'You are suppose to read his lips.' He then looks at a watch called the Ross Perot Watch and notices that it isn't running; the sales clerk tells him 'It runs, it doesn't run, it runs, it doesn't run...' He then notices a watch called the Bill Clinton Watch and sees that it runs, has hands and looks like a pretty good watch. He asks the sales clerk how much. The sales clerk replies, '$19.95 plus tax, plus tax, plus tax, plus tax, plus tax...'

George Bush and Hillary Clinton are alone on an elevator. Hillary grabs the STOP button and pulls it out, stranding the pair between floors. She strips off her clothes, throws them to the floor and cries, 'George, make me feel like a woman!'

Bush strips off HIS clothes, throws them to the floor, and says, 'Fold those.'

One day, President Clinton was walking around Washington DC wondering how on earth he was going

to fix the mess the country is in. Seeking inspiration, he decided to pay a visit to several of the monuments and memorials of the great presidents of old.

First, he stops off at the Washington Monument and there he meets and talks with the spirit of President Washington. 'George,' he says, 'you were one of the best leaders our country ever had. You really helped get this country off to a good start and provided clear direction for the people. Everybody trusted you – how can I gain the trust of the people?'

President Washington looked at President Clinton and said, 'Never tell a lie.' Clinton thought this over, frowning, and walked on. After a while, he came to the Jefferson Memorial and there talked with the spirit of Thomas Jefferson. 'Tom,' said Clinton, 'You were also one of our greatest founding fathers, and you helped construct the basis for our entire legal system. You helped to pass really good laws and you were very popular as a president. How can I improve my popularity?' President Jefferson looked at President Clinton and said, 'Never raise taxes.' Clinton winced and walked away muttering to himself.

Finally, he came to the Lincoln Memorial. Feeling a little desperate now, he pleads with the spirit of President Lincoln. 'Abe,' he says, 'You were undoubtedly one of the greatest Presidents we've ever had. You were a man of great integrity and you really helped pull our people together and establish unity after the Civil War.

Also, you abolished slavery, and in doing so you helped to set all of our people free from an uncivilized institution. How can I help to set our people free today?' President Lincoln looked at President Clinton and said simply, 'Go see a play.'

Clinton is on the beach at Martha's Vinyard and finds that an old bottle has washed ashore. When the President opens it a very pale genie snakes out.
Genie: Hi Bill, I'm a very weak genie so I can only grant you one wish and it had better be easy if you want me to do it.
Clinton: I pray for world peace, give me that.
Genie: That's a little hard, give me something easier.
Clinton: Make Hillary into the most beautiful woman in the world?
Genie: World peace it is then.

Bill Clinton was carrying a live turkey down the street when a man walks up and says, 'Where did you get that turkey?'

The turkey replies, 'I don't know, he just picked me up.'

Candidate Clinton was stumping for votes one day and at the end of his speech he exhorted everyone to vote for him.

'Not me,' came a voice from the back.

'Why not?' asked Bill.

'Because my father was a Republican, and his father before him, and by God, I'm going to vote Republican, too!'

'That's no way to think,' retorted Bill. 'What if they were all liars, adulterers and drug addicts?'

'Well then, I guess we would all vote Democratic.'

A man is hitchhiking prior to the election; a car slows and the driver asks, 'Who are you voting for this November?'

The hitchhiker replies, 'Bush,' and the car speeds off.

It's a very hot day, with very few cars passing. The hitchhiker feels it's time for more pragmatic politics. Another car slows, this time driven by a very attractive young woman. She asks, 'Who are you voting for come November?'

The hitchhiker replies, 'Clinton,' and the young woman says 'Get in.'

After some time, as they drive along, the woman begins loosening her clothing and making all sort of invitations. The hitchhiker gets very nervous. The

woman notices his nervousness and asks what is the matter. The hitchhiker replies 'Well, I've got a confession to make: I've only been a Democrat for 20 minutes and already I feel like screwing somebody.'

Bill was driving in the mountains when he went too fast around a curve and found his car teetering on the edge of a sheer drop. The President was thrown through the windshield and was balanced precariously on the hood of the car. He didn't dare breathe lest the car become unbalanced and crash onto the rocks below. A few minutes later, an average American voter came along in a pickup truck with a long rope in the back. Bill hoarsely whispered, 'Help me, help me. The car may go at any moment and I'll die if you don't help.'

The voter said, 'What?' Bill said, 'If I move, both me and the car are going over the cliff. I need you to either throw me the rope and pull me to safety, or sit on the back bumper of the car so I can crawl off of here.' The voter did neither and a gust of wind came and blew the car over the cliff.

Another voter happened by and had just heard the end of the exchange between the two men. 'Why didn't you save him? Didn't you hear him?'

The voter with the rope replied, 'Yeah, I heard him. But you know how he lies...'

Bill was complaining to Hillary about cutting the White House staff. 'If you would learn to iron, we could do without the ironing lady,' he suggested.

Hillary replied, 'If you learned how to make love, we could do without the gardener!'

Al Gore and Bill Clinton were discussing pre-marital sex. Al asked Bill, 'I never slept with my wife before we were married, did you?' Bill replied, 'I'm not sure, what was Tipper's maiden name?'

In a meeting with the Pope, Clinton was arguing his pro-abortion stance. Clinton finally asked the unwavering Pope, 'Your holiness, you mean to tell me you can see no possible reason in the world where abortion is the right choice?' The Pope looked Clinton in the eye, thought for a second and said, 'Yeah, maybe one, but it's about 50 years too late.'

The doctor gave Hillary the news, 'You're pregnant!' Hillary called Bill on the phone, gave him the news, and screamed, 'Why weren't you using a condom?'

Bill replied, 'I ALWAYS use a condom! ... Who is this, anyway?'

Bill and Hillary are standing on top of a burning 30-story building. Because of the height of the building ladders are unable to reach the first couple on the top of the building. The firefighters get out their net and yell to the Clintons they they will have to jump if they are to be saved. Hillary pushes Bill aside telling him 'I must jump first.'

Bill gawks and asks why. Hillary explains that if he jumps first and she dies in the flames that it will be impossible for him to run the country without her help. Bill, seeing the wisdom of this, agrees. So, with a smile of triumph, Hillary throws herself over the edge to the awaiting net below. About the time she reaches the fifth floor on her way to the bottom the firemen pull the net away. Hillary, screaming, crashes to her death on the pavement. The firemen, smiling proudly to one another, yell up to Bill, 'Come on Mr President, jump, we will catch you in the net.' Bill, feeling thoroughly impressed with his own intelligence, yells to the firefighters, 'No way! I saw what you guys did to Hillary. Put the net DOWN, then I'll jump!'

The Pope and President Clinton are sitting together on a plane. The Pope says, 'Hey, want to hear a good President Clinton joke?'

Clinton says 'But I'm President Clinton!'

The Pope replies, 'Oh, that's OK. I'll tell it slow.'

Bill Clinton, Ross Perot and George Bush are on the *Titanic* while it's sinking. Bush says 'Get the women and the children off.' Perot says, 'Screw the women and children – we have to get off!'

Clinton says, 'Do we really have time?'

Tony Blair goes to Ireland and asks Bill Clinton what he thinks about the Northern Ireland position.

'Gee, I haven't tried that one before,' Bill replies.

Bill Clinton said on the news last night that he was ready to take Saddam Hussein out. Saddam replied saying that it was okay as long as he didn't have to sleep with him.

One day I was walking along a dock and on one side I saw Bill Clinton drowning. On the other side, I saw Hillary drowning. I had a tough decision to make. Should I have a burrito or a cheeseburger for lunch?

Once Bill Clinton visited an elementary school to talk to a group of 3rd graders. He said to them, 'Today we are going to discuss the difference between a tragedy, a

great loss and an accident.' Then he said, 'Can anyone give me an example of a tragedy?' A little boy raises his hand and says, 'If a kid runs out in the street after a ball and gets hit by a car?'

Clinton says, 'No, that would be an accident. Can anyone else try?'

A little girl raises her hand and says, 'If a busload of kids drove off a cliff?'

Clinton says, 'No, that would be a great loss. Come on, anyone else?'

A boy raises his hand and says, 'If you and Mrs Clinton was on a plane and it blew up?'

Then Clinton says, 'Well, yes, but can you tell me why it would be considered a tragedy?'

And the little boy says, 'Well, it wouldn't have been an accident, and it sure as heck wouldn't have been a great loss.'

One day, Clinton called the White House interior decorator into the Oval Office. He was furious and said, 'Chelsea is very upset because she thinks she has the ugliest room in the entire White House; I want something done about it immediately!'

'Yes Sir, Mr President,' the interior decorator replies. 'I'll take those mirrors out right away!'

Clinton received a letter from a man who said he would break his legs if he bothered his wife one more time. Clinton goes to Al Gore for advice and asks what he ought to do. Gore says, contact the man and promise never to see the man's wife again. Clinton says, 'I can't, the guy didn't sign his name.'

Bill Clinton and Chelsea are walking along a beach in California. Summoning up all the courage a father can, he asks, 'Chelsea, how is college going, socially? Do you have any, uh, boyfriends, and are you being, uh, nice?'

Chelsea thinks for a second, then replies, 'Well Dad, if you're asking me "Am I having sex?" well, the answer is no, not as YOU define it.'

The President was awakened one night by an urgent call from the Pentagon. 'Mr President,' said the four-star general, barely able to contain himself, 'There's good news and bad news.'

'Oh, no,' muttered the President, 'Well, let me have the bad news first.'

'The bad news, Sir, is that we've been invaded by creatures from another planet.'

'Gosh, and the good news?'

'The good news, sir, is that they eat reporters and piss oil.'

Barbara Bush to Hillary Clinton: 'Your daughter's so ugly Woody Allen wouldn't touch her.'

A caddy who had been working a golf outing that had the President, OJ Simpson, Ted Kennedy and Paula Jones in the same group was sitting in the locker room with his head down running his fingers through his hair. Joe, one of the other caddies said, 'You look bad. Was your group any good?'

'No!' Joe said. 'It took forever to complete the round.'

'What was the problem?' his friend asked. 'Didn't they play well?'

'No,' Joe said, 'their game has not improved any.'

'What do you mean?'

'Well Paula Jones is still hooking, OJ was slicing, Ted Kennedy was still in the water, and Clinton was trying to improve his lie.'

A woman calls the White House on the phone. Hillary Clinton answers. Hillary says, 'Sorry, mam, this is not the National Weather Service.'

President Bill hears the short conversation and asks, 'Who was that?'

Hillary says, 'Oh, some gal asking if the coast was clear.'

Bill's Legacy: Americans can be assured of one thing after this administration leaves office: They won't rename any White House sleeping quarters the 'Clinton Bedroom'.

Q: Bill Clinton divorces Hillary and is dating three women. He wants to marry one of them but can't decide which one. He gives them each $1,000. The first one spends $800 on clothes and puts the other $200 in the bank. The second one spends $200 on clothes and puts $800 in the bank. The third one puts the whole $1,000 in the bank. Which one does he marry?
A: The one with big tits.

Clinton's New Bumper Sticker: If you see Air Force One a-rockin', don't bother knockin'.

Bill Clinton: Fancy a quickie?
Hillary: As opposed to what?

Al Gore says to Bill: 'You should close your curtains at night. Last night I saw Hillary making love through the living room window.'

'Ha, ha,' says Bill. 'The joke's on you. I wasn't even home!'

It was reported on Sunday morning that Clinton's Chief of Staff, Erskin Bowls, approached the President with some news.

'Mr President,' he began, 'I am afraid I have some bad news, good news and some bad news for you.'

'Give it to me in order,' requested the President.

'The bad news is that a picket demanding your impeachment is in front of the White House,' said Erskin.

'What is the good news?' asked the President.

'Well,' said Erskin cautiously, 'there is only one so far.'

'That's not too bad,' said the President, 'what could be so bad about that?'

'It's Gore holding the sign.' said Erskin.

Hillary wins $100 million on the national lottery and calls home to tell Bill. 'I won the lottery. Start packing!'

'What should I pack? Where are we going?' replies Bill, looking forward to a few weeks in the sun.

'I don't care,' replies Hillary. 'Just be out of there when I get home.'

Bill comes home early one day and finds Hillary in bed with Bob Dole. 'What are you doing?' he shouted.

'See?' she says to Dole. 'Didn't I tell you he was dumb?'

Bill Clinton picks up a girl in a bar and asks her to come to his apartment. She says, 'I'd love to, but I'm on my menstrual cycle.'

'Oh, that's OK,' Bill replies. 'We can put it in the trunk.'

One day, Chelsea Clinton asked her dad, 'Do all fairy tales start with "Once upon a time"'?

Bill answered, 'No, some start with "After I'm elected. . ."'

Short, Stubby, Bendy Ones

Q: Bill and Hillary are on a sinking boat. Who gets saved?
A: The nation.

Q: Did you hear that someone threw a bottle of beer at Clinton?
A: Yes, but it's OK. It was a Draft and he was able to dodge it.

Q: What is the difference between Dan Quayle, Bill Clinton and Jane Fonda?
A: Jane Fonda went to Vietnam.

Q: What is the difference between George Washington, Richard Nixon, and Bill Clinton?
A: Washington couldn't tell a lie, Nixon couldn't tell the truth, and Clinton doesn't know the difference.

Q: What will Bill Clinton be known for when compared with other presidents?
A: The president after Bush.

Q: Why does Bill Clinton have a clean conscience?
A: Because it's never used.

Q: Which of Monica Lewinsky's body parts does Bill Clinton most enjoy looking at?
A: The top of her head.

Q: What is Monica Lewinsky's favorite item in her wardrobe?
A: Knee Pads.

Q: What is the difference between Bill Clinton and yoghurt?
A: Yoghurt has culture.

Q: What is Bill Clinton's definition of safe sex?
A: A padded headboard.

Q: Why did Hillary marry Bill?
A: Because a vibrator can't mow the lawn.

Q: Why does Bill Clinton walk round with his zipper open?
A: Just in case he has to count to eleven.

Q: How can you tell if Bill Clinton is dead?
A: He stays stiff for more than two minutes.

Q: What is Clinton's favorite Olympic sport?
A: Skating on thin ice.

Q: Why does Bill Clinton have a pet name for his penis?
A: Because he wants to be on first name terms with the person who makes 90 per cent of his decisions.

Q: What is the definition of the word B.I.T.C.H.?
A: Bill's In Trouble Call Hillary.

Q: How do you brainwash Bill Clinton?
A: Give him an enema.

Q: What does Bill say to Hillary after having sex?
A: 'Honey, I'll be home in 20 minutes.'

Q: What do you get when you cross a crooked politician with a dishonest lawyer?
A: Chelsea.

Q: Why did Monica Lewinsky refer to Bill Clinton as the 'snowstorm'.
A: Because she didn't know when he was coming, how many inches she'd get or how long he'd stay.

Q: Why is the Clintons' lovemaking fast and furious?
A: He's fast, she's furious.

Q: What tune does the band play when Clinton enters the room?
A: 'Don't Inhale to the Chief'.

Q: What does Teddy Kennedy have that Bill Clinton wishes he had?
A: An ex-wife and a dead girl friend.

Q: What's the difference between Bill Clinton and the *Titanic*?
A: Only 1600 people went down on the *Titanic*.

Q: What's the difference between Hillary Clinton and a pit bull?
A: The pit bull doesn't carry a briefcase.

Q: How many Bill Clintons does it take to change a lightbulb?
A: HE DOESN'T! He whines a while, says 'I feel your pain', and gets congress to pass a billion dollar light security bill, and blames Republicans and special interests for not making lightbulbs free.

Q: Why does Bill Clinton wear underwear?
A. To keep his ankles warm.

Q: What kind of neckwear does Hillary Clinton look best in?
A: A noose.

Q: Why has the crime rate been reduced by half in Arkansas?
A: Bill Clinton took all the crooks with him to Washington D.C.

Q: What's pink and smells like Flowers?
A: Bill Clinton's face.

Q: What has Bill Clinton got in common with Burger King?
A: Whoppers!

Q: Why is Chelsea Clinton a miracle child?
A: Because lawyers use their personalities for birth control.

Q: What kind of jewellery does Hillary look best in?
A: Handcuffs.

Q: What is the Secret Service's codename for President Clinton?
A: Monica's harmonica.

Q: What position did Monica Lewinsky have at the White House?
A: Missionary.

Q: What's the difference between Vince Foster, Ron Brown and Monica Lewinsky?
A: Monica is the only one who took a shot in the head from Bill and lived to tell about it.

Q: Why doesn't Monica eat bananas?
A: She can't find the zipper.

Q: How does Bill rationalize that oral sex is not a sexual relationship?
A: Because Monica didn't swallow.

Q: What do Hillary Clinton and J. Edgar Hoover have in common?
A: They're both female impersonators.

Q: Why do they call him slick willy?
A: He uses K-Y Jelly.

Q: What did Hillary tell Bill when the Paula Jones story broke?
A: 'You idiot. I TOLD YOU to let Teddy Kennedy drive her home!'

Q: What's the definition of an Arkansas Virgin?
A: A girl that can run faster than the Governor.

Q: What's the difference between Bill Clinton and a catfish?
A: One's a bottom feeding scum-sucker and the other is a fish

Q: Why is Bill Clinton so interested in events in the Middle East?
A: He thinks the Gaza Strip is a topless bar.

Q: What are the two worst things about Bill Clinton?
A: His faces.

Q: Why is Bill Clinton apprehensive about going to the movies?
A: Because he's afraid the usherette will ask to see his stub.

Q: If Bill and Hillary jumped together off the Washington monument, who'd land first?
A: Who cares?

Q: What's President Clinton's favorite card game?
A: Pokeher.

Q: Why is Hillary supporting Bill?
A: She needs him in office to give her a pardon.

Q: How many full time White House staff members does it take to screw in a light bulb?
A: None, they make the interns do all the screwing.

Q: How did Bill Clinton get a crick in his neck?
A: Trying to save both faces.

Q: If Bill and Hillary and Al and Tipper took a boat ride and the boat capsized, who would be saved?
A: The United States of America.

Q: What's the best place to photograph Clinton Administration officials?
A: A police lineup.

Q: Why did Bill Clinton cross the road?
A: To tax the chicken.

Q: What's the difference between Bill Clinton and an elephant?
A: About 20 pounds and a jogging suit.

Q: What will future analysts of his Presidency say was Clinton's primary dysfunction during his second term?
A: Premature Evacuation.

Q: What advice did Yasser Arafat give President Clinton?
A: 'Bill....Goats don't talk!!'

Q: What was the first thing Monica saw in government?
A: The Executive Branch.

Q: Why does Hillary Clinton wear high collared blouses?
A: So you won't see her Adam's apple move when Bill talks.

Q: In Arkansas, what is the new use they found for sheep?
A: Wool.

Q: What is the difference between Bill Clinton and Jimmy Carter?
A: Jimmy Carter waited until after the inauguration to break his promises.

Q: What is the only thing worse than an incompetent liberal President?
A: A competent liberal President.

Q: Who are the three most dangerous women in the White House?
A: 1. Monica Lewinsky with a lawyer
2. Hillary Clinton with a theory
3. An intern with a chipped tooth

Q: What does Bill Clinton have in common with former great Presidents?
A: Absolutely nothing.

Q: What's the President's favourite party game?
A: Swallow the leader.

Q: What do you get when you give Bill Clinton a penny for his thoughts?
A: Change.

Q: Why did Bill Clinton get his new dog Buddy?
A: So when he is in the Oval Office and Hillary hears him say, 'Lie down on the floor, roll over on your back and I'll give you a bone' Hillary thinks he is talking to the dog.

Q: Why did the chicken cross the Atlantic?
A: To attend the D-Day celebrations.

Q: Why is Chelsea growing up a confused child?
A: Because Dad can't keep his pants on and Mom wants to wear them.

Q: What do Bill Clinton and Kurt Cobain have in common?
A: Half a brain and Gore on their backs.

Q: What is the difference between Whitewater and Watergate?
A: No one died in Watergate.

Q: Why won't there be a White House Christmas pageant this year?
A: They can't find three wise men and a virgin.

Q: What is the favourite nursery rhyme of Clinton's bimbos?
A: Humpme Dumpme.

Q: What is Bill's definition of safe sex?
A: When Hillary is out of town.

Q: Have you read Hillary's new book?
A: It Takes a Village to Satisfy My Husband.

Q: Why are Nixon and Clinton alike?
A: They were both brought down by Deepthroat.

Q: What does Hillary Clinton have in common with Gerald Ford?
A: They both became president without being elected.

Hillary Wouldn't Like It

Bill Clinton is in the Lincoln bedroom engaged in some heavy foreplay with Monica, when he decides that it's time to finish the deed. As he's doing so, Monica lets out a cry of discomfort. 'What's the matter, honey?' asks the President.

'I'm still a virgin, and it hurts!' was the reply. Bill responds, 'I feel your pain!'

WASHINTON DC NEWS REPORT:
In the aftermath of the initial administration responses to the breaking story, it seems apparent that Mr Clinton has left a bad taste in Lewinsky's mouth. A growing majority are finding the President's story hard to swallow, noting that it appears quite evident that Monica was influenced by some sort of presidential 'gag order'. The First Lady, the recognized steward of the President's power base, is reported to be afraid that Lewinsky has blown everything. Vernon Jordan is reported to have suggested that Ms Lewinsky approach the President with a stiff upper lip for the time being, and is quite upset at how much damage her wagging tongue seems to have done.

It is said that Bill Clinton is considering changing the Democratic Party emblem from a donkey to a condom, because it stands for inflation, protects a bunch of pricks, halts production and gives a false sense of security while being screwed.

Bill to Monica: 'I didn't tell you to lie in deposition ... I told you to lie in THAT position!'

Q: Why did Buddy, the President's dog, call a press conference?
A: To announce he was going to have the President neutered.

Q: What's the difference between Bill Clinton and a pickpocket?
A: A pickpocket snatches watches.

Q: What does Hillary Clinton do after shaving her pussy in the morning?
A: She puts a suit and tie on him and sends him off to work.

Q: What is Monica Lewinsky's favorite instrument?
A: Well, she's pretty good on the piano, but she sucks on the organ.

One day, Bill Clinton is at the White House and has to attend to the call of nature. He finds himself in the restroom at a urinal next to Jesse Jackson. He peeks down into the next urinal and is astounded at the size of Jackson's organ. 'Damn, Jesse, how in the world did you get such a huge dick?' he asked. 'Well, uh, Bill, each night before I go to bed, I whack it on the bedpost. That's how I got it so big.' Jackson replied.

So that night as he is preparing for bed, Bill Clinton, still amazed at the sight of Jesse Jackson's organ, decides to try out the bedpost bit, and whacks his dick on the post. The noise rouses Hillary, who says 'That you, Jesse?'

Q: What's the difference between Hillary Clinton and the Tundra?
A: The Tundra gets drilled once in a while.

Bill asks a cheerleader out. Her response: 'Mr President, if you can raise my skirt as high as you've hiked our taxes, if you can get your dick as hard as you've made our lives hard, if you can screw me like you've screwed the American people, then I'll go out with you!'

Q: How do you know Bill Clinton has finished having sex?
A: When you have to wipe the 'White-Water' off your blouse...

Q: What's the difference between Hugh Grant and Bill Clinton?
A: One's a bad actor whose career went down the toilet after he got caught out after getting a blow job. The other was the star of *Four Weddings and a Funeral.*

Nixon was the crooked President who followed Johnson.
Clinton is the sitting President with a crooked Johnson.

There was a game show on TV every week, in which a special guest had 10 questions to discover what the mystery item was. So one week the host introduces the special guest and it's none other than Hillary Clinton. The audience are delighted as the host sits Hillary down on a chair and blindfolds her.

Then just before he pulls back the curtain on this weeks mystery item, he takes a look at what it is, as he doesn't know himself. He nearly dies of embarrassment when he sees it's a horse's dick. Thinking quickly, he decides to go ahead since it's a live show. So he draws back the curtain and the audience cracks up laughing. The host say to Hillary, 'Can we have your first question.'

Hillary replies, 'Could you eat it?' And the host mumbles a bit and says, 'Er, well, I, er suppose you could. What's your next question Hillary?'

Hillary replies, 'It wouldn't happen to be a horse's dick, would it???'

The Clintons and the Gores were very stressed out and decided to rest at Camp David. That night they were all sitting around the fire, Hillary then suggested that they should partner-switch. The others were very reluctant, but Hillary talked them into it. The next morning Hillary was at the table, reading the news-

paper, when Bill came down. Bill got a glass of juice out of the fridge and asked, 'Hill, how was the night?' She said it was the best night she had ever had and that she had 20 orgasms. Bill's face fell. Hillary, after going into detail with Bill, finally asked, 'Oh, how was your night with Al?'

At a news conference, a journalist said to President Clinton: 'Gennifer Flowers has said publicly that you have a small penis. Would you please comment on this.'

'The truth is,' said Bill, 'that she has a big mouth.'

Q: What do White House interns and the Bermuda Triangle have in common?
A: They both swallow a lot of seamen.

Q: What's the difference between Watergate and Fornigate?
A: We know who Deep Throat is this time.

Q: What's the difference between President Clinton and O.J. Simpson?
A: It only took 12 jerks to get O.J. off.

The number of presidential aides required to change a light bulb depends on the President.

Nixon: Only one to change the light bulb but five to go out in the middle of the night and steal the light bulb. Then nine to lie and cover up for the five who got caught stealing the light bulb.

Ford: Three to select the study committee, nine to sit on the study committee, five to review the study committee's report, one to shelve the report.

Carter: The President went out himself and purchased a dozen bulbs at a discount, then he changed the bulb himself. Then it took three people to write the press release, two to apologize for violating union rules, and five union electricians to put back the old burned out bulb.

Reagan: One to shoot out the old burned out bulb with a 45. Then a carpenter, a plasterer and an electrician to replace the fixture.

Bush: Twenty five to smuggle cocaine from Colombia and divert the profits to light bulb purchase. Three to launder the excess funds. Two to explain that the President was out of the loop.

Clinton: One to give the President a blow job while he changes the light bulb.

Bill suddenly realised he could wrap up early, what with the UK, France and China asking him to hold off bombing Iraq for a few days more, so he took a stroll through the corridors of power. He came across this young secretary and suggested a drink. After a high-ball, she took him into the study for a mammoth BJ session, then let herself out. Bill went to his drawer and took out a chalk bag and rubbed his hands in it furiously.

With his hands behind his back to walked into his private quarters to find Hillary standing there glaring at him. 'Where the HELL have you been until this hour?' she demands to know. 'Well, I bumped into a young secretary and we had a drink, since then she's been on my dick in the study for the last three hours.' Hillary grabs his hands and studies them. 'You lying son-of-a-bitch, you've been bowling!'

The Clinton Files

Top Ten Reasons Why Bill Clinton Dodged the Draft

10. He wanted to hang out with Dan Quayle.
9. He was allergic to Vietnamese food.
8. He thought 'gook' meant the stains on Gennifer Flowers' panties.
7. He wanted to do one better than Gary Hart.
6. He had his weekly appointment with a hooker that day.
5. He needed some good scandals for when he ran for presidency. Soon we'll be hearing about how he smoked marijuana with his brother.
4. He heard there were no women in the army, and he wasn't too into Oriental chicks.
3. He was against the whore. Oops, I mean war.
2. When they said sign, he thought they meant a subscription to *Penthouse*.
1. He had to weigh his priorities...mow down the Vietcong or mow down Gennifer Flowers' lawn.

Top Ten Unusual Comments on Monica Lewinsky's Intern Performance Report

10. Truly an eager beaver.
9. Uses too much teeth.
8. Stays late, comes early.
7. Excellent oral dictation skills: has never missed a period.
6. Great attitude! Willing to accept a heavy load.
5. Frequently complains of jaw pain.
4. Although not a whiner, tends to be a moaner.
3. 'In box' is always clean and shiny.
2. Tends to blab on the telephone.
1. This intern may suck, but she doesn't inhale.

Top Ten Names Clinton has for his Penis

10. The White House Staff
9. His Tiny Advisor
8. The Nuclear Button
7. The Executive Branch
6. The Little Pollster
5. His Soft Contribution
4. His Pocket Veto
3. The Secret Servicer
2. The Presidential Caucus
1. Little Rock

Two Cows (A comparative study of Governments and Religions)

IF A...

COMMUNIST has two cows, he gives both to the government and the government sells him some of the milk.

SOCIALIST has two cows, he gives both to the government and the government gives him some of the milk.

NAZI has two cows, the government shoots him and takes both cows.

CAPITALIST has two cows, he sells one and buys a bull.

LIBERAL has two cows, he sells them to the rich, then taxes them on one cow and gives it to the poor.

CONSERVATIVE has two cows, he locks them up and charges people to look at them.

PACIFIST has two cows, they stampede him.

HILLARY CLINTON has two cows, she robs the ranches and gives everyone 2 cows. If she doesn't have enough, she gives them bull.

BILL CLINTON has two cows, he makes sure a few Arkansas Highway Patrolmen are outside the door when it happens.

Top Ten Cool Things About Having an Affair with the President

(from *The Late Show* with David Letterman)

10. At request, nuclear launch code change to '90210'.
9. Your old job: beautician at strip mall. Your new job: Secretary of Commerce.
8. You now belong to a select group of 48,000 women.
7. Allowed to drive the rarely seen Presidential van.
6. Get to pick up the red phone and scream, 'What's happenin', you Ruski bastards?'
5. You're the only college student to arrive at Spring Break in a B1 bomber.
4. Your name: Kate. Name of scandal: Kategate.
3. According to Constitution, your 15-year-old brother automatically becomes 'First Dude.'
2. Every morning, a delicious continental breakfast prepared by Al Gore.
1. 50% off at all participating McDonald's.

Top Ten White House Valentine's Day Poems

10. How do I love thee? Let me count the entries in the visitors' log.
9. Monica, Monica, quiet young mouse – taking her Bill to the floor of the House.
8. Hi there! Happy Valentine's day! Sorry to serve your subpoena this way.
7. Roses are red, then they turn gray, My heart goes pitter-pat when you wear that beret.
6. Shall I compare thee to my high school drama teacher?
5. Twinkle, twinkle, Kenneth Starr, I talked to Vernon in the car. I promised him my lips are sealed, but I'll change my mind, for a sweet book deal.
4. As soon as I'm finished bombing Iraq, I'd like to get you in the sack.
3. Will you, on the night in question of February 14th, be my Valentine?
2. Violets are blue, Roses are thorny. All hell breaks loose, when Bubba gets horny.
1. I'll bomb England, I'll bomb France, if you'll remove my underpants.

The Top Sixteen Nicknames for the Presidential Scandal

16. Lolitagate
15. Quick! Time For Another War With Iraq!
14. The Crook, The Intern, The Wife, and that 'Hey Vern' guy
13. The D Cup Domes Scandal
12. Starr Wars
11. Ex-intern killed in freak missile accident-gate
10. The Lay of Pigs
9. Stain of the Union Undress
8. Monicaca
7. 'Paid for by Gore/Rodham 2000'-gate
6. Pubic Missile Crisis
5. Linguapalooza
4. Honey, I shrunk my approval rating
3. Gaining-On-Wilt-gate
2. Tail to the Chief
1. Bad Will Hunting

Top Ten Benefits From a White House Internship

10. First-hand knowledge of domestic affairs
9. Pay is lousy, but the hush money is great
8. Gives new meaning to MTV slogan 'Rock the Vote'
7. Observe the President's commitment to young people first hand
6. Learn intricacies of statutory rape law
5. Have President chase around desk brandishing his 'subpoena'
4. President tells you he really wants you on his staff
3. Try out JFK's legendary rocking chair
2. Have president introduce you to his 'special investigator'
1. Find out what a politician means when he says he's been polling his constituents

Top Ten Lines from Monica Lewinsky's Resume

10. Served as one of only 12 presidential handlers
9. Many interns put out press releases for staff; I put out for the President
8. Acted as White House affairs liaison
7. Scheduled President's comings and goings
6. Designed Clinton statue; Chaired erection committee
5. Defined and tested Clinton's 'No Fly Zone'.
4. Assisted Commander in Chief in sending seamen into active duty
3. Debunked story that Lincoln Bedroom was reserved for political favors
2. Maintained President's in box
1. Raised Clinton's poll standing

Top Movies Based on the Monica Lewinsky Story

101 Depositions
Affair to Forget
All the President's Members
All the President's Women
As Wood As It Gets
Big Hair, Big City
Blowing My Way
Blown out of the White House
Cleavage and Butt-Head Do America
Days of Wine & Bozos
Deep Throat II
Dial M For Phone Sex
Down and Out in Beverly Hills and Washington DC
Executive Privilege
Fatal Attraction
Forrest Hump
Four Blow Jobs & an Impeachment
Free my Willy
Going Down on the Titanic
Good Bill Hunting
Guess Who's Coming After Dinner
Lady and the Scamp
Liar Liar 2
Look Who's Sweating Now

My Spare Lady
Nightmare at 6900 Pennsylvania Avenue: Toothless People
Phallus in Wonderland
Sex, Lies & Audiotapes
Shaft
6900 Pennsylvania Avenue
Silence of the Ma'ams
Swallow the Leader
Terns of Impeachment
That Thing You Do
The American 'Vice' President
The First Wives Club
The Fly
The French Connection
The Johnson Administration
The Lyin' King
The Magnificent Semen
The Nine Commandments
Truthless People
White House Guys Can't Hump
White House Nights

Top Ten White House Jobs That Sound Dirty

(from *The Late Show* with David Letterman)

10. Polishing the Presidential Podium
9. Unwrapping the Big Mac
8. Taking Buddy for a walk
7. Handling the hotline
6. Vacuuming under the Oval Office desk
5. Waxing Air Force One
4. Shaking hands with the French Ambassador
3. Giving the President an oral briefing
2. Taking dictation
1. Polling

What Clinton Says and What He Really Means

I was not lying.	I was standing up and she was lying.
It wasn't adultery.	She wasn't even an adult.
I did not have oral sex with her.	She was having it with me.
It is time to get on with the nation's business.	If this isn't off the front page by tomorrow, I'm bombing Iraq.

The Top Fifteen Graffiti Sayings in the White House

15. Mute Newt!
14. The toilet paper can't be reached, and I'm about to be impeached
13. This is my veto, this is my cane. This one's fer sell-'n, and this one's fer lay'n
12. If you think love is blind call the Justice Department . . . Ask for Janet
11. Kenneth Starr does it in his briefs
10. Flush twice; it's a long way to Congress
9. George Washington slept here... but we're still waiting for the check!
8. Bubba Slept Here... and here... and here...
7. Whig Party Rulz 4ever!!!
6. Here I sit, broken hearted – my welfare bill has been discarded
5. Paula exaggerated
4. Clinton is a potatoe head!
3. If your missile is having a crisis, call Marilyn at 555-3621
2. Buddy Sniffs Butts
1. Here I sit all broken hearted, wish that Intern's lips had never parted!

The Top Sixteen Chelsea Clinton Pet Peeves About College

16. Every time she cuts her 8am class, CNN switches to a live feed from the lecture hall.
15. PoliSci textbook only contains pictures from her 'dumpy' years.
14. Social life hampered by mandatory Secret Service body cavity search of potential dates.
13. No room in dorm for all those boxes of missing Whitewater documents.
12. Daddy won't sign the Cafeteria Food Reform Bill.
11. No one wants to waste good pot on a Clinton.
10. Steamy makeout sessions usually end with the guy getting his ass kicked by the Secret Service.
9. Tipper no longer around to clean up after her and Socks.
8. Every boy who hits on you winds up on a 'peace-keeping force' in Bosnia within 48 hours.
7. Constant comparisons to notable Stanford alum Ted Koppel usually refer to physical resemblance.
6. Bourbon shots not free like the ones 'Uncle Ted' serves back home.

5. Drunken frat boys always confusing her with Amy Carter.
4. Football coach keeps begging her to get Janet Reno to enroll.
3. RA's write you up if the Chinese Delegates stay past midnight.
2. Anatomy lab cadaver none other than Al Gore.
1. The man makes 200 grand a year – you'd think he could bring his own weed when he visits.

NEW COMPUTER VIRUS ALERT...

PAT BUCHANAN VIRUS: Your system works fine, but complains loudly about foreign software.

COLIN POWELL VIRUS: Makes its presence known, but doesn't do anything. Secretly you wish it would.

HILLARY CLINTON VIRUS: Files disappear, only to reappear mysteriously a year later, in another directory.

O. J. SIMPSON VIRUS: You know it's guilty of trashing your system, but you just can't prove it.

BOB DOLE VIRUS: Could be virulent, but it's been around too long to be much of a threat.

POLITICALLY CORRECT VIRUS: Never identifies itself as a 'virus', but instead refers to itself as an 'electronic micro-organism'.

ROSS PEROT VIRUS: Activates every component in your system, just before the whole thing quits.

DAN QUAYLE VIRUS: Their is sumthing rong with yur koputer, but ewe cant figyur outt watt!

OLLIE NORTH VIRUS: Causes your printer to become a paper shredder.

GEORGE BUSH VIRUS: It starts by boldly stating: 'Read my docs...No New Files!' on the screen. It proceeds to fill up all the free space on your hard drive with new files, then blames it on the Congressional virus.

BILL CLINTON VIRUS: It feels your pain, humps your computer before making your hard drive turn into software

Ten Things You Should Never Say if You Meet Bill Clinton

1. Hello, I'm Gennifer Flowers
2. Hello, I'm Paula Jones
3. How's the tattoo?
4. So, how exactly did Vince Foster die?
5. So, what was Vietnam really like?
6. Have you ever made it with Madeleine Albright?
7. Mr President, I feel your pain
8. John Major loves to watch Chelsea score
9. Do you want to go whitewater rafting?
10. Name me ten things you and Ted Kennedy have in common

(from *The Unofficial Book of Political Lists*, Robson Books 1997)

Quotes

'Change, change, change...That's all we'll have in our pockets if Bill Clinton is elected president.'

George Bush

JFK: 'Ich bin ein Berliner.'
Nixon: 'I am not a crook.'
Reagan: 'Tear down that wall, Mr Gorbachev.'
Clinton: 'Suck my dick.'

'Our good friend, a man I admire deeply, former President Jimmy Carter has been hospitalized for the treatment of a skin rash. He's gonna be fine, but if any Democratic president came down with a skin rash, I think it'd be Clinton.'

Jay Leno

'Hillary Clinton may be the First Lady, but she certainly isn't the last.'

Anonymous

'The problem is that Clinton swore to tell the truth, the whole truth and nothing but the truth. But to Clinton, those are three different things.'

Jay Leno

'After spending $30 million dollars investigating Clinton Kenneth Starr finally found a smoking gun. It turned out to be in the President's pants.'

Jay Leno

'It came out today that Clinton once tried to have phone sex with Hillary but she said, 'Not tonight, I have an ear ache."'

Jay Leno

'Scandal in the Wind: Bill Clinton's alleged affair with a White House intern means Al Gore 'is now just an orgasm away from the presidency.'

Jay Leno

'Monica is considering suing the president. She wants $1 million for pain and suffering, and $2.50 for dry cleaning.'

Jay Leno

'Hillary Clinton said that while the President was testifying in the Paula Jones case she was doing some household chores. Little things like sewing the President's pants to his shirts.'

Conan O'Brien

'Sleeping with the President used to mean that you attended a Reagan cabinet meeting.'

Anonymous

'President Clinton apparently gets so much action that every couple of weeks they have to spray WD-40 on his zipper.'

David Letterman

'Some of the women he's been with have actually said that the President told them that oral sex is not a sin according to the Bible. What Bible has he been reading? Definitely not the King James version. He got the Rick James version.'

Keenan Ivory Wayans

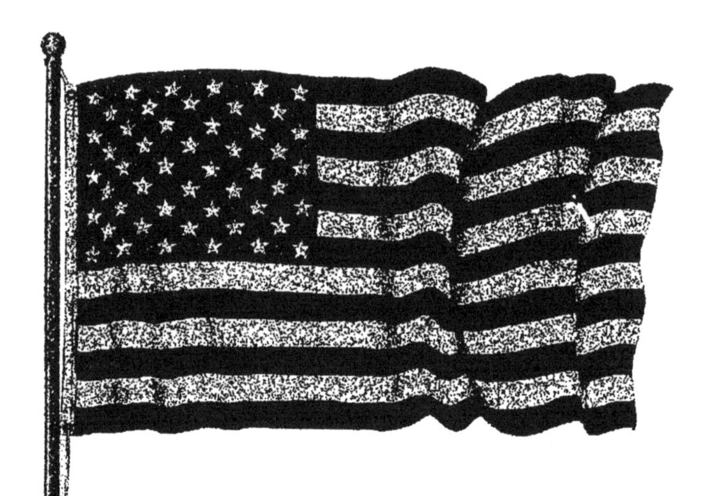

Campaign Slogans & Bumper Stickers

Smell my lips.....No more Bush

It's still the economy. And he's still stupid

Honk if Bill Clinton says you're rich!

First Hillary, Then Gennifer, Now US

Aides can give you sex

Go ahead make my lay

Honk if you haven't had sex with Bill Clinton

I feel your tonsils

If she didn't spit, you must acquit

If Vince Foster had had a gun in his hand, he wouldn't be dead today

It isn't sex unless you smoke a cigarette

Monica Lewinsky has a big mouth

The Sex Education President

The Wicked Witch of the West Wing

Bumper sticker on Arkansan car:
If you can read this You're not from here

Abort Clinton

Impeach the President...And her husband, too!

Where the Hell is Lee Harvey Oswald When We Need Him?

Clinton Doesn't Inhale – He Sucks

Carter is no longer the worst US President

Hey Hillary! Shut-up and redecorate!

My other car was cancelled by the Clinton Tax Bill

You can't shit here, 'cause your asshole's in the White House

Hillary sucks, and we all know who

Clinton Health Care: A Trojan Hearse

BILL CLINTON – Why stupid people shouldn't vote

The jokes over, bring back Bush

We Need Character, not Characters in the White House

Honk If You Want an Adult in the White House

Clinton/Gore '96 – Let's Spend the Next Generation's Money!

Clinton-Gore '96 – The Administration with convictions ... And more coming every day!

Chelsea Has Two Mommies

Inhale to the Chief

You voted for change ... That's all you'll have left

Two terms for Clinton ... One in office, one in jail

Voting Republican means never having to say you're sorry

Hillary Happens

At least Gennifer got kissed

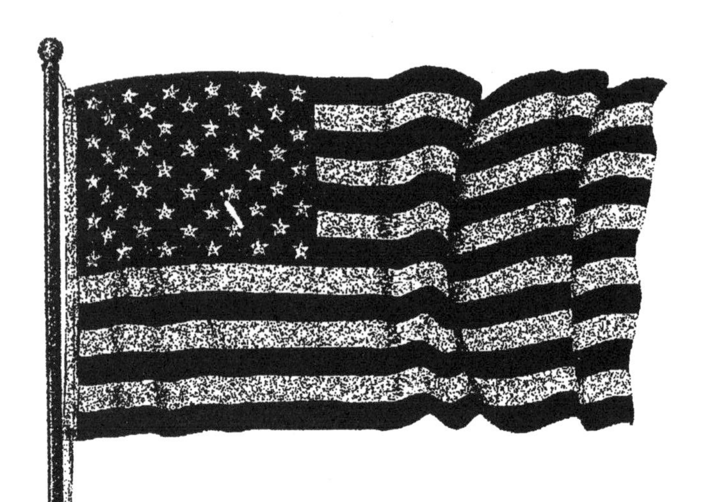

Clinton's Iambic Pentameter

A high-minded couple called Billary
In assets took more than their fillery.
If their name were Nixon
The press would be fixin'
To stick their fair necks in the pillory!

STARR I ARE –
a newly discovered tale of Dr Seuss

I'm here to ask
As you'll soon see –
Did you grope
Miss Lewinsky?

Did you grope her
In your house?
Did you grope
Beneath her blouse?

I did not do that
Here or there –
I did not do that
Anywhere!

I did not do that
Near or far –
I did not do that
Starr-You-Are.

Did you smile?
Did you flirt?
Did you peek
Beneath her skirt?

And did you tell
the girl to lie
When called upon
To testify?

I do not like you
Starr-You-Are –
I think that you
Have gone too far.

I will not answer
Any more –
Perhaps I will go
Start a war!

The public's easy
To distract –
When bombs are
Falling on Iraq!

Can't pity the President's plight.
It's sure self-inflicted all right.

A sexual vandal,
He'll always court scandal,
To conservative critics' delight!

There once was a leader from Hope
Who financed his elections with dope.
And then later he wailed,
'I never inhaled,
And I always thought hemp was just rope.'

The President's loud protestation
On his fall to the intern's temptation:
'This affair is still moral,
As long as it's oral.
Straight screwing I save for the nation.'

A Polish girl interned for Bill
And soon she was eating her fill.
Said her friend, 'Don't you fear
That some trouble is near?'
Said the girl, 'No, I'm taking the Pill.'

A Right Wing Conspiracy Plan

Now stories in DC are rife,
With rumors of Bill's private life.
Trouble is brewing.
He won't stop his screwing,
And none of it's with his dear wife.

They say that his member is bent.
Such talk of the President!!
But none can agree
To what degree,
And in which direction it went.

If you've ever seen Hillary's pan,
It's hard to place blame on the man.
But as to his member,
She cannot remember.
It's never been part of her plan.

For the Pres. oral was prefrential.
The scene didn't look presidential,
The Chief was quite pleased,
To have the Aide on her knees,
In a shot that would prove consequential.

Old Bill had his hand on her head.
He looked in her eyes and he said,
'I feel like a winner,
And not a real sinner.
Can you sing me a song while you're fed.'

She nodded and broke into song.
She sang like nothing was wrong,
In a spectacular manner,
The Star Spangled Banner,
While keeping both lips on his dong.

And then there's the stain on the dress,
That's put Bill under some stress.
Should he deny it,
The facts sure imply it,
Her mouth couldn't hold the excess.

Or was it a whole different matter?
Dismissed as being tabloid tatter,
Was the President wearing,
The dress she was sharing,
Crossdressing while spilling his batter?

For an intern she's a hell of a girl.
Bill told her, 'It's only a whirl,
And I'll never confess,
To this whole nasty mess,
If ever your lips do unfurl.'

Now Slick is a real miracle man.
The polls show if anyone can,
He can stick it in double,
And come out of trouble,
It's a Right Wing conspiracy plan.

Bill Clinton's Favourite Things
(to the tune of 'My Favourite Things' from
The Sound of Music)

Blow jobs and land deals in backwater places,
Big Macs and french fries and girls with big faces,
Lots of nice cleavage that makes willie spring,
These are a few of my favourite things

Susan McDougal and Gennifer Flowers,
Horny young interns who while 'way the hours,
Profits from futures that Hillary brings,
These are a few of my favourite things

Beating the draft board and getting elected,
Naming to judgeships some hacks I've selected,
Conspiracy theories that blame the right wing,
These are a few of my favourite things

Golfing with Vernon and suborning perjury,
Falling down drunk that required knee surgery
Stars in the White House who come here to sing
These are a few of my favourite things

Meeting with Boris and Helmut and Tony,
States of the Union with lots of baloney,
Winning debates and the joy of my flings,
These are a few of my favourite things

When that Jones bites,
When Ken Starr stings,
When I'm feeling sad,
I simply remember my favourite things
And then I don't feel so bad